I AM AN EMPATH
Energy Healing Guide for Empathic and Highly Sensitive People

BY JOSHUA MOORE

FREE DOWNLOAD

INSIGHTFUL GROWTH STRATEGIES FOR YOUR PERSONAL AND PROFESSIONAL SUCCESS!

TABLE OF CONTENTS

I Am an Empath is a book about managing emotional anxiety, and using intuition to benefit from this sensitivity in your everyday life. You have the potential to make the most of being in tune with your emotions and understanding the feelings of people around you. This book is different from others of its kind because it gathers information from various perspectives in order to provide a comprehensive look at empathy as a spectrum of experience; rather than a personality trait that one simply has or does not have.

I Am an Empath is for anyone in search of ways to turn emotional sensitivity into strength of intuition that is applicable in any setting. It will benefit those who already find themselves to be empathically aware, as well as individuals looking to develop a more empathetic lifestyle.

In this book, you will find information on:
- Common Traits of Empathic Individuals
- Understanding Empathy, Having Empathic Tendencies, and Identifying as an Empath
- Personality Type as an Empathy Indicator
- Benefits and Challenges of Being Empathic
- Empathetic Self-Protection
- Stress and Anxiety Reduction Strategies
- How to Balance Your Empathy
- Developing an Empathic Practice
- How to Deal with Narcissistic Individuals

If you're ready to unlock the possibilities of your empathic experience, learn to manage stress and anxiety, navigate personal relationships, and balance your emotional sensitivity, then purchase **I Am an Empath.**

Begin your journey to a fulfilling life of awareness and support today!

Introduction

I have a student and good friend who we'll call Laura. She is shy and soft-spoken, observant and incredibly sensitive. I don't mean to say that she's easily offended, or you have to watch what you say around her for fear of being rebuked or judged for your opinion. But Laura has this ability to pick up on subtle connections between people, and finishes others' sentences more often than could be chalked up to coincidence. For this reason, she is easy to talk to and conversations with her tend to feel like they cover incredible distance in a matter of moments. She is the first person I confide in when I have a problem or don't know how to emotionally respond to a situation, and she always has an answer to help me figure it out.

Laura is very creative and loves listening to music. I've never met a dog who wasn't obsessed with her, and her bedroom could be considered a botanical garden, due to the vast number and variety of plants she takes care of. Laura doesn't eat meat and hates violent movies. When we disagree on something, she shrinks slightly and drops her voice down to a whisper, which makes me feel guilty for raising mine on occasion. She can be moody at times and gets bored easily with repetitive tasks. You may as well not ask her to do things she doesn't like to in the first place, because it bums her out

—

so much that she's likely to never finish at all. Laura is incapable of telling lies and is therefore terrible at poker. However, she is the master of a perfectly timed hug and, I can spend days hanging out with her.

Yet, Laura is different around large groups of people. The few times we've gone to parties or concerts together, she almost seems like a different person upon walking into a crowded room or loud music venue. She gets jumpy and won't stop whipping her head around, as if someone is sneaking up behind her, or looking over her shoulder. Her posture crumbles and she stares at the ground. It's difficult to talk to her in these situations and I hate to see her this way. I often try to help but can never make it past the armor she's put up until hours later, when it's quiet and she has some control over her surroundings again.

Laura has recently discovered a word to explain this kind of behavior, and realizes there are many others like her. She calls it being Empathic, and says the common characteristics of these types of individuals match hers with incredible accuracy. Since this discovery, Laura has been able to talk to others about her emotional sensitivity and learned how to better express the way she feels in certain situations. She says she wishes everyone like her knew this stuff.

If you relate to Laura in any one of the ways that

make her the unique and sensitive person she is, you might be empathic, too. Consider this book as my way of trying to make up for all those helpless moments when I didn't know what to say to Laura to make her feel better. I used to think that it was something she had to figure out alone; but through the education and growth that have followed her discovering the name of this faceless cloud of overwhelming emotions, I've also learned that there are things you can do to manage them. You can help prevent anxiety attacks from happening in the first place, and the people around you can actually help in real and tangible ways.

The fact of the matter is, nobody experiences this journey of life in exactly the same manner. Some people are simply more sensitive than others, but the results of this sensitivity are as complex as it gets. It's easy to view this overwhelming emotional overload as some kind of curse meant to keep you from living a normal and happy life. In reality, it is possible to live with and, in spite of your empathic tendencies, even benefit from them.

Being empathic means you have the gift of being in tune with the emotions of others, and can even experience them as your own. It means you have the ability to heal anxiety and calm emotional turbulence. It could even mean communicating with forces much greater than yourself, which is an awesome and sometimes frightening responsibility. It means you've been given the opportunity to connect with people in a way few others can, and that it may take some training and focus to make the most of it.

The good news is that you're definitely not alone, and you've encountered this book to help you along your journey of empathic enlightenment. In the coming pages, you'll learn to describe your sensitivity and categorize the abilities that come along with it. You'll find it has more to do with personality type than you might think, and learn why you might be attracted to some people more than others. And of course, you'll get specific solutions and techniques for managing your emotions, reducing stress and anxiety, and finding the balance to maintain a fulfilling and joyful lifestyle; whether you're talking to a single friend or interacting with a room full of people.

Overview

Part I: So You Think You're an Empath

1. Common Traits of Empathic Individuals

This series of questions will help you gauge where you might fall on the empathy spectrum, based on your level of sensitivity towards a number of topics or ideas. There is no scoring system, as the questionnaire is made up of simple "yes" or "no" choices and is strictly dependent on your total number of each.

2. Understanding Empathy, Having Empathic Tendencies, and Identifying as an Empath

Learn to differentiate between these terms, which are closely related but can represent very different ways of experiencing emotions and external stimuli. Also discover the terminology that will help you to categorize your sensitivity by specific abilities you may or may not have; and visualize where that might place you on the empathy spectrum.

3. Personality Type as Empathy Indicator

Included is an in-depth discussion of each of the 16 personality types according to the Myers-Briggs Type Indicator (MBTI), and how they potentially relate to a person's capacity for empathy. Learn how the MBTI works and visualize where you might fall, based on the psychological preferences that govern the exam. Discover the advantages and obstacles each personality type might face in managing their empathy, as well as when relating to the sensitivity of others.

Part II: Solutions for the Empath in You

4. Benefits of Being Empathic

Learn to see your emotional sensitivity as a gift rather than a curse through this description of positive aspects that can lead to an enriching and fulfilled empathic life experience.

5. Challenges of Being Empathic

Prepare yourself for the possible obstacles someone with empathic tendencies might face in managing

---

their sensitivity, and consider initial solutions for dealing with each. Realize that a positive outlook can transform these challenges from impossible road blocks to doable opportunities that will enable you to grow into a stronger person.

6. Empathic Self-Protection

A discussion of how to navigate relationships as an empath, touching on family and best friends; good friends and acquaintances; and co-workers and classmates. Recognize the importance of distinguishing between these three groups, based on your needs and responses to individual people in your life.

7. Things to Keep in Mind (and Body)

A list of things to remember when managing the effects of your emotional sensitivity, and explanations of how to apply them in your everyday life. Explore methods of confronting your pain, learn the importance of self-esteem, and discover tactics for reducing your discomfort in general.

8. Stress and Anxiety Reduction Strategies

Learn specific strategies to deal with anxiety attacks and emotional episodes. Discover short-term and long-term solutions for each, and live a comfortable life through your sensitivity. Topics covered here include setting emotional limits, grounding techniques, and outlets to keep your mind busy in situations of information overload.

9. How to Balance Your Empathy

A discussion of possible approaches to maintain an emotional balance in between episodes, and how to reduce the frequency of their occurrence. Examples include nurturing an awareness of your body and developing a sense of emotional immunity.

10. Put Feeling to Empathic Practice

Suggestions for helping others develop their empathic tendencies, including specific examples for friends, family, and children. Discover how to become more empathic if you find yourself on the other end of the spectrum, and explore methods of walking a mile in someone else's shoes.

---

11. How to Deal with Narcissistic Individuals

A short overview of what it means to be a narcissist, how to recognize them in relationships, and possible ways of dealing with these difficult people without being taken advantage of.

Common Traits of Empathic Individuals

By now there's a pretty widely accepted list of general personality characteristics that are shared by many Empathic people. You don't have to relate to every single one, or even most of them, to be considered as having a large potential for Empathy. Some people find that only a few of these traits are applicable to them, but they are felt so strongly that it still "counts". Chances are good that if you find yourself reading this book, you're aware of certain feelings or experiences that have led you to believe you are a highly sensitive empath. Here's a series of questions that, if answered honestly, should help to clarify your belief or dispel any speculations you might have in deciding how empathic you are:

1. **Are you highly creative and imaginative?**

2. **Do you feel a deep connection to nature?**

3. **Does eating meat gross you out?**

4. **Are animals and children generally attracted to you?**

5. Are you free spirited and drawn to adventure, travel, and freedom?

6. Are you bored or distracted easily?

7. Do you find it difficult or impossible to tell a lie?

8. Is it difficult to complete a task when your heart isn't in it?

9. Are you a caring and nurturing person by nature? Do you feel compelled to care for others in need?

10. Is it difficult or unbearable to witness the sight of violence and cruelty?

11. Will you inconvenience yourself in order to avoid interpersonal conflict?

12. Are you prone to multiple and intense mood swings throughout the day?

13. Do your thoughts feel sluggish in a messy room?

14. Are you in tune to the flow of energy in a space and do you know how to correct it?

15. Do you experience a hyper-awareness of your surroundings without necessarily trying to?

16. Are you particularly aware of other peoples' or animals' (even plants') suffering and pain?

17. Are you intolerant of narcissism and disappointed by a large ego?

18. Do you have strong intuitions and seem to know things without any prior experience of a particular person or situation?

19. Are you usually looking for answers or an explanation to why something happened?

20. Does this ever lead to an overwhelming overload of information?

21. Are you a sharp judge of character and do you tend to see through other people's intentions?

22. Would you consider yourself as having an addictive personality?

23. Do you distract yourself from overwhelming anxiety or pain with substances or obsessive activities (exercise, yoga, etc.)?

24. Have you gone to the doctor for persistent digestive and/or lower back problems?

25. Are you naturally drawn to/interested in holistic therapy and supernatural phenomena?

26. Do you feel connected to another plane of existence that others don't seem to be aware of?

27. Do you prefer new objects and clothing over recycled belongings?

28. Have you ever felt what seems like the residual energy of a previous owner?

29. Do you find yourself particularly moved by someone else's emotions?

30. Do people tend to open up to you about a problem or dilemma they're having?

31. Has anyone ever expressed a feeling of lifted weight or tangible relief after having this kind of conversation with you?

32. Have you ever felt heavier, cloudy, or physically sore after having this kind of conversation with someone else?

33. Have you ever experienced physical pain in the presence of someone who's ill, or even from a distance if a loved one is sick?

34. Do you experience mental and physical fatigue, especially after spending time in large groups of people or social situations?

35. Do you feel the need to "recharge" through a period of solitude after these types of experiences?

36. Does it seem like you are always absorbing the general mood of a group of people, or the collective community in general?

37. Do you get that "Friday feeling" even if it's your day off?

38. Do Sundays and Mondays come with a heavy sense of dread even without obligations on these days?

39. Have you ever been physically ill or felt an incurable anxiety in concurrence with a public tragedy or natural disaster?

As you can see, there's a spectrum when it comes to the scope of these characteristics. Towards the beginning they seem to be the simple personality traits of a sensitive individual, yet, as the questions progress, there's a definite transition towards being effected on a larger scale and with greater intensity. This is because a person's capacity for empathy is not black and white – there are many different combinations and levels of traits associated with this facet of human emotion and experience.

Now that you've got a better idea of how "much" you really feel (or don't), we're going to break down these attributes in order to understand the difference between various kinds of empathy and the spectrum of its effects on a person.

Understanding Empathy; Having Empathic Tendencies; Identifying as an Empath

While the three statements above may seem like different ways of saying the same thing, they're actually important distinctions to make when it comes to empathic traits and effective solutions.

Understanding Empathy is simply having the capacity to share the feelings of another person. It is the most common form of empathy, and is a personality trait almost all people have, excluding narcissists. This is what we mean by the saying, "walk a mile in someone else's shoes" or considering things from another person's specific point of view. This can also be referred to as the ability to **recognize** another person's emotional state, **relate** to that state, and **feel or show the appropriate concern** in response.

Having Empathic tendencies means to psychologically identify with a particular feeling, thought, or emotion of someone else's. It's characterized by the direct experience of an external stimulation, and is usually the kind of sensitivity responsible for mood swings or anxiety. These tendencies can be purely cognitive; being able to consider divergent perspectives from our own, or they can be causes of personal distress through emotional contagion, which is literally experiencing someone else's feelings.

An individual who has empathic tendencies is sometimes classified as a **Highly Sensitive Person (HSP)**, defined by a condition known as **Sensory Processing Sensitivity (SPS)**. This results in a hypersensitivity to external stimuli, a greater depth of cognitive processing, and/or advanced emotional reactivity. A high measure of this personality trait is responsible for someone's identification as an HSP. There are legitimate personality tests that can tell whether this category applies to you, but there are some common examples shared by most people who identify as such.

Highly Sensitive People might:
- Be overwhelmed by bright lights, strong smells, etc.
- Get anxious when busy or feel under pressure
- Have an aversion to violence
- Be introverted and require solitude to recharge
- Avoid upsetting situations and conflict
- Be especially moved by art and music
- Have a complex inner life that doesn't manifest itself in social situations
- Be shy and reserved by nature
- Have a low tolerance for physical pain
- Be aware of subtleties in their immediate environment

- Get startled/surprised easily
- Have difficulty multitasking
- Resist lifestyle changes

Identifying as an Empath is usually different than merely having empathy or showing empathic tendencies. An **Empath** is a person with the ability to comprehend the mental or emotional state of another individual or group of people. This is an extremely rare condition that very few individuals experience in full capacity. It is specifically characterized by the term clairsentience, which is the distinction between an awareness and direct experience of someone else's feelings and emotions. While being an Empath may seem like having superpowers, it's a gift that comes with a heavy price. Empaths have an incredible potential for being emotional healers and helping other people confront their anxieties; this also puts them in a position of extreme vulnerability, and it takes years of training and focus to develop even a small amount of control over their abilities. Empaths have been around forever, and were even revered as spiritual and otherworldly advisors in some ancient cultures. The Native American Heyoka, or "Sacred Clown" was said to play the role of an emotional mirror, showing others their faults and weaknesses, and could also provide guidance to resolving these issues. Some researchers believe that we are all born as empaths, but lose the ability to tune into others' emotions through societal conditioning. Regardless of their source, there are eight types of empathic capabilities. While very few people

—

experience all or even a majority of them in one lifetime, any combination of one or two could mean you identify as an empath.

#1 Claircognizant
<u>Definition:</u> The intuitive knowledge of right and wrong without concrete evidence or research; as well as the ability to see through others' lies and misinformation.

<u>Benefits:</u> An accurate moral compass and guide; able to know who is trustworthy.

<u>Setbacks:</u> May feel resistance at knowledge through "gut feeling"; as a potential invasion of privacy; they have an inability to shut off.

#2 Emotionally Receptive
<u>Definition:</u> The ability to physically feel another's emotions with no outward expression or explanation.

<u>Benefits:</u> Able to give accurate support, provide healing solutions.

<u>Setbacks:</u> Draining of energy; confusion about source of anxiety; possible resistance/suspicion from other person.

#3 Physically Receptive
<u>Definition:</u> Capacity to share someone's illness or bodily pain, due to an intuitive analysis or connection between loved ones.

Benefits: Capable of emotional support and energetic healing; knowledge of safety from a distance.

Setbacks: Physical pain and exhaustion.

#4 Fauna
Definition: A natural inclination towards/attraction to animals.

Benefits: Gives a voice to those who can't speak themselves.

Setbacks: Possibility of acknowledging pain without knowing how to fix/cure it.

#5 Flora
Definition: Characterized by a sensitivity towards plants.

Benefits: Gardening skill, intuitive understanding of ecology.

Setbacks: Possibility of acknowledging pain without knowing how to fix/cure it.

#6 Ecological Intuitive
Definition: The ability to feel energy signals transmitted by the Earth, as the result of a sensitivity to nature.

Benefits: Ability to observe the occurrence of a natural disaster.

Setbacks: Feeling of helplessness, insignificance compared to the scale of pain/problem.

#7 Incident Intuitive
Definition: The ability to see how an event or interaction will play out, based on making connections between people and their perceived emotions and actions.

Benefits: Ability to prevent conflict.

Setbacks: Feeling of helplessness; unable to "shut off".

#8 Social Intuitive
Definition: The capacity to read a person's unexpressed thoughts by picking up on body language and/or emotional distress

Benefits: Able to understand what someone means, regardless of difficulty with language/expression.

Setbacks: Invasion of privacy, knowing things you didn't necessarily want/need to be aware of.

The simple chart below illustrates the possible spectrum of empathic categorizations and the relative abilities that may come with each. There are infinite variations within the spectrum, as manifestations of this sensitivity are different in everyone. The purpose here is only to provide a way of visualizing where you might find yourself

---

as a result of how many times you answered "yes to the questions above. The more "yes's" you have tallied by the end of the questionnaire, the further to the right of the chart you may be located.

SELF-IDENTIFICATION TABLE

Identifying as a Narcissist	Disregard for feeling of others	Obsession with self	
Understanding Empathy	Recognize / Relate to emotion	Feel / Show appropriate concern	
Having Empathic Tendencies	Emotionally Receptive	Physically Receptive	
Highly Sensitive Person	Sensory Processing Sensitivity	Claircognizant	Fauna / Flora Communication
Identifying as an Empath	Ecological Intuitive	Incident Intuitive	Social Intuitive

For the purposes of this book, we'll be focusing mostly on the large, middle section of the Empathy spectrum which consists of those individuals who may not have paranormal abilities; but who could very well be Highly Sensitive People with a more reactive emotional disposition than the average person. All of the information will also be useful to those wishing to understand the minds and emotions of someone with Empathic tendencies a little better, or even help a clairsentient Empath manage their overwhelming condition, with some of the same methods as their more common counterparts. The most important thing for anyone, regardless of their capacity for empathy, is to find a balance between allowing yourself to feel emotions as a necessary part of existence, without letting your sensitivities and anxiety get in the way of leading an enjoyable and productive lifestyle. For this reason, knowledge of the entire spectrum rather than your own particular place on its path is valuable information that will help anyone to understand how easy or difficult managing Empathy might be for someone else.

Here are some important takeaways:

- A person doesn't have to identify with every common trait associated with being empathic to identify as an Empath.

- Empathy is measured on a spectrum from simple, observable, and common personality traits all the way to seemingly spiritual abilities.
- **Understanding empathy** is the ability to recognize another person's emotional state, relate to that state, and feel or show the appropriate concern in response.
- All people, with the exception of narcissists, have the capacity to understand and experience empathy in some sense.
- **Empathic tendencies** represent an ability to psychologically identify with a particular feeling, thought, or emotion in someone else.
- There is a vast spectrum of empathic tendencies, which can range from picking up on the collective mood in a room full of people to acknowledging specific feelings and emotions in another individual.
- An **Empath** is a person with the ability to comprehend the mental or emotional state of another individual, or group of people. These kinds of people are characterized by the distinction between an awareness and direct experience of someone else's feelings and emotions, also known as clairsentience.
- There are eight categories of empathic capability, each of which is a rare gift

as well as a source of incredible vulnerability. These abilities are all related to energy healing in some way, and require extensive training and focus to manage.

Personality Type as Empathy Indicator

We've all taken a personality test at one point or another, and there are hundreds to choose from online that can help us understand ourselves a little better. What you might not have considered is the correlation between an individual's personality type and their capacity for empathy. In this section, I'll be using the 16 categories defined by the **Myers-Briggs Type Indicator (MBTI)** as a starting point for a discussion of different types of people, their natural relationship to empathy, and suggested ways to either emphasize or improve their initial preference in order to be as balanced as possible. (This information can be found at http://www.myersbriggs.org/my-mbti-personality-type/mbti-basics/.)

The MBTI is an introspective questionnaire that is designed to indicate psychological preferences in how an individual perceives the world and makes decisions. It's broken down into four areas; each with two possible results:

Introversion/Extroversion: A measure of sociability and how you interact within large groups. A person with high levels of empathy is most often an introvert who needs time alone to recharge after social situations.

Sensing/Intuition: This relationship refers to how

---

someone processes data. Sensing is focused on facts and concrete proof, while Intuition relies on the recognition of patterns and impressions. People who have a preference towards sensing over intuition will generally have a harder time feeling empathy as the logical counterpart to an imaginative intuition-based processor.

Thinking/Feeling: Refers to how people make decisions. Thinkers tend to be rational and objective, and may have difficulty connecting with others on an emotional level. Feelers are naturally empathetic and gentle, but are also easily hurt due to their vulnerability to emotion.

Judging/Perceiving: Measures the preference between order and spontaneity. The least relevant category in terms of empathy, someone with a preference towards judging might feel anxiety from a loss of control, whereas someone with a tendency toward perceiving may end up feeling trapped in plans or situations they aren't interested in.

	Sensing←		→Intuitive	
→Judging Introvert↑	ISTJ – Examiner	ISFJ – Defender	INFJ – Confidant	INTJ – Strategist
→Perceiving↓	ISTP – Craftsman	ISFP – Artist	INFP – Dreamer	INTP – Engineer
	ESTP – Persuader	ESFP – Entertainer	ENFP – Advocate	ENTP – Originator
Judging↓ Extrovert↓	ESTJ – Overseer	ESFJ – Supporter	ENFJ – Mentor	ENTJ – Chief
	Thinking←	→Feeling←		→Thinking

ST – Directing SF – Relating NF – Valuing NT – Visioning

Above is a visualization of how each of the 16 personality categories is related to the four areas of psychological preference. I recommend taking a variation of the Myers-Briggs Type Indicator before proceeding to the explanations below, as it will give you a point of contrast from which to read about each type as it relates to you.

Before we get down to the in-depth exploration of each category, it's important to note that these are only generalizations, and cannot possibly accommodate every single type of person's specific needs or preferences. While it will probably help to take some variation of the test yourself in order to see where you might lie on the spectrum, by no means does a certain categorization condemn you to a certain way of thinking or feeling. It's best to keep an open mind and take this kind of information with a grain of salt.

ISTJ (introversion/sensing/thinking/judging) – Examiner

Definition: The ISTJ personality type is also known as the Examiner. Examiners are generally quiet, serious, and dependable, practical and responsible. They make a logical plan and stick to it with consistency and determination.

Advantages: This type of realistic understanding makes Examiners surprisingly caring individuals who are great at expressing sympathy towards others. It's easy for them to see why a particular problem or situation would bother somebody, and therefore will be supportive in finding a solution.

Obstacles: As ISTJs naturally prefer logic over emotion, they may face resistance when placing themselves in another person's shoes. While they will actively listen to loved ones in need and be as supportive as they can, it may be more difficult to totally comprehend what that person is feeling emotionally. Because of this, a little extra effort is required for an Examiner to overcome their natural tendency towards logic and allow themselves to be truly aware of their own emotions.

ISFJ (introversion/sensing/feeling/judging) – Defender

Definition: ISFJs are called Defenders for their loyal and conscientious nature. They are observant and concerned with the feelings of others. Defenders strive for order and harmony at home and work, as well as in personal relationships.

Advantages: Defenders are empathetic individuals who are very capable of understanding the emotions of others. All they really want is to make their friends happy! They are very adept at sensing when someone is upset and will try to fix things however they can.

Obstacles: Because of their natural concern for the happiness of others, Defenders can sometimes forget about their own feelings and find themselves in a place of emotional neglect. An ISFJ would never want to bother their friends because they know that everyone has troubles of their own, and would do well to remember that asking for help is not a sign of weakness.

INFJ (introversion/intuition/feeling/judging) – Confidant

Definition: INFJ is the personality type of the Confidant, a person who is always looking for meaning and connection in ideas and relationships. They are truly curious about the motivations of other people and would like to organize everyone's talents for the common good.

Advantages: Confidants are naturally empathetic, and talented when it comes to finding connections between the emotions of others. They are often capable of picking up on the feelings of those close to them and can quickly find the relationship between a person's physical actions and what they're feeling on the inside. The Confidant is familiar with putting him- or herself in somebody else's shoes and is always available to listen to a friend in need.

Obstacles: The INFJ's ability to listen and absorb another person's feelings may leave them feeling like they are in over their heads at times. The ease in which they're able to empathize with someone else's emotions can result in difficulty finding solutions, and Confidants are prone to letting the anxiety of others' affect them more than it should. Every Confidant needs someone they, in turn, can trust to ease the burden of these emotions they so willingly take on without complaint.

INTJ (introversion/intuition/thinking/judging) – Strategist

Definition: INTJs are Strategists with original minds and big ambitions. They quickly see patterns in actions and events, and develop informed perspectives from a distance. They have high standards of competence for themselves and others.

Advantages: The Strategist is highly observant and able to read a person's body language without a literal explanation of how they're feeling. They are notoriously self-aware and capable of protecting themselves from emotional distractions.

Obstacles: The tendency of an INTJ to favor logic over all else is responsible for their difficulty understanding an emotional reaction as the proper response to any given situation. Their focus on awareness of the self can make it difficult to consider the feelings of others, and they need to learn to support the idea that not everyone can be as rational as they are.

ISTP
(introversion/sensing/thinking/perceiving) –
Craftsman

Definition: ISTP signifies the persuasion of the Craftsman, a quiet observer who is quick to find workable solutions. They are efficient and practical, as well as proponents of logical organization.

Advantages: Craftsmen (or women) are independent and capable of handling their own emotions without the help of anyone else. They are able to understand why someone might be upset and possess the skills necessary to help.

Obstacles: The Craftsman's independence is a gift and a curse in the way that they expect everyone to be able to manage their feelings as well as they do. While ISTP's are aware of their ability to help someone in need, they are shrewd judges of what is worth their time and may choose to let that person fend for him- or herself. Giving someone the benefit of the doubt may prove to help a Craftsman see the value in using their talents to help others.

ISFP
(introversion/sensing/feeling/perceiving) –
Artist

Definition: ISFP's are dubbed the Artist personality type due to their friendly and sensitive nature. They live in the moment and enjoy being involved in what's going on around them. Artists are free spirits who like to make their own schedule and will avoid conflict if at all possible.

Advantages: There is an attentive listener in the ISFP, and they are often able to sympathize with the emotions of their friends and family. The Artist has a great capacity for empathy due to

---

their sensitivity for feelings and imagination.

Obstacles: Although Artists feel very deeply, they are not always able to translate the specifics of these emotions from abstract thought to literal action. It's easy for them to see a situation from someone else's perspective, but sometimes struggle to find the right words of support and comfort. The Artist type should remember that a practical solution can indeed deliver concrete results.

INFP
(introversion/intuition/feeling/perceiving) —
Dreamer

Definition: The INFP or Dreamer is idealistic and very loyal to their values and loved ones. They are curious and open-minded, quick to try out a new idea and highly adaptable to unfamiliar situations.

Advantages: The imaginative Dreamer can easily place him- or herself in someone else's shoes. They are capable of empathy in their determination to understand the people who are important to them, and are patient enough to cultivate this understanding.

Obstacles: While they may not experience the natural ease of understanding emotions like some other personality types, their dedication and loyalty make up for it. It can take a good

---

deal of conscious effort and focus to achieve the awareness they strive for, and they will succeed as long as they don't give up on their companions.

INTP
(introversion/intuition/thinking/perceiving) – Engineer

Definition: A person who identifies as an INTP is said to be an Engineer. They are constantly searching for knowledge and understanding through logical explanation. They are more interested in the development of their ideas than in social interaction.

Advantages: Engineers are so wired to solve problems that they can find themselves aware of others' emotional struggles without any verbal expression from the other party. They are extremely intelligent and easily able to rationally empathize with the way someone is feeling in any given situation.

Obstacles: Even though an INTP reaches an easy understanding of others through the calculation of known variables, they may have trouble suggesting relevant emotional solutions to someone else's problems. If the Engineer allows him- or herself to tap into the feelings beneath their sound logic, they are more than capable of connecting to others on an emotional level.

ESTP
(extroversion/sensing/thinking/perceiving) —
Persuader

Definition: The ESTP is a born Persuader; flexible and tolerant with a pragmatic approach focused on immediate results. They prefer action over theory when it comes to solving problems. Persuaders enjoy the time they're able to spend with other people.

Advantages: Persuaders will take the time to truly empathize with the people they care about. They value personal connection and will go to great lengths to ensure they're available to help their friends and family. The practiced ESTP is also able to shut off this sensitivity when they need to protect their own emotions.

Obstacles: Persuaders can find it hard to see the benefit of constantly connecting with the emotions of others, especially if there's no visible advantage for them to stick their neck out. If they're not consciously aware of their tendency towards logic, Persuaders can ignore someone else's feelings due to a lack of interest rather than malicious intent.

ESFP
(extroversion/sensing/feeling/perceiving) —
Entertainer

Definition: Known as the Entertainer, an ESFP personality type it outgoing and friendly. They love life, people, and working with others to make things happen. Flexible and spontaneous, they adapt to new environments well.

Advantages: Entertainers are genuinely compassionate people who just want everyone to have a good time. They are great at showing compassion for others, especially when they've been through a similarly tough situation or have some familiarity with a particular set of emotions.

Obstacles: Despite their natural draw towards tenderness, an ESFP may have difficulty experiencing advanced levels of empathy in dealing with feelings and situations they have not personally encountered before. However, their willingness to help the ones they love can often give them the patience to overcome this setback and utilize the emotions they feel on such a deep level.

**ENFP
(extroversion/intuition/feeling/perceiving) –
Advocate**

Definition: ENFPs are natural Advocates. They are warm, enthusiastic, and imaginative, with the ability to make connections between events and information very easily. Advocates are the first ones to give affirmation and support to anyone, not just their friends and family.

Advantages: Due to their extremely caring and open-minded nature, Advocates are capable of a unique kind of empathy. Their vivid imaginations allows an ENFP to see things from another's perspective without much effort, and are capable of understanding a variety of situations, thanks to their wealth of first-hand experience. They tend to give great advice and loving support, whether they were asked for it or not.

Obstacles: Although the ENFP is compassionate and aware of others, they are usually more aware of their own emotions as a default. In order to reach their true empathic potential, it will take constant focus and determination in getting past this natural inclination towards themselves.

ENTP
(extroversion/intuition/thinking/perceiving) – Originator

Definition: Originators are of the ENTP persuasion, resulting in a clever and outspoken personality. They are resourceful and strategic, having a knack for reading the expressions of other people. Originators are bored by routine and don't like to sit still for very long.

Advantages: The clever disposition of the ENTP makes it easy for them to connect body language with what someone else is feeling at any given moment. They are adept at understanding the perspective of others due to their alert awareness and have the potential to turn this into emotional empathy.

Obstacles: Just because an Originator is able to understand the emotions of another person doesn't mean they will choose to respond in a similar way. Favoring logic over sensitivity, the Originator requires patience in taking the time to really see things from another's point of view.

ESTJ (extroversion/sensing/thinking/judging) – Overseer

Definition: ESTJs, otherwise called Overseers, are practical and realistic individuals. They are efficient and organized, and prefer to systematically devise a plan and stick to it decisively. They have a clear set of standards, which they hold themselves and others to keeping.

Advantages: As naturally caring people, Overseers have a desire to tend to the practical needs of their loved ones and can often come up with a specific solution to any given problematic situation. They have the capacity to understand where someone else is coming from, especially if they've experienced something similar.

Obstacles: Despite their desire to protect the ones they care about, the ESTJ's preference of efficiency and logic over emotions can make it difficult to express true empathy. In order to really put themselves in someone else's shoes, they must remember why a person is important to them and realize it's worth the effort of understanding how they feel.

ESFJ (extroversion/sensing/feeling/judging) – Supporter

Definition: The Supporter exhibits characteristics of the ESFJ personality type, which are associated with warm intentions and a cooperative nature. They are determined to help develop harmony in their immediate environment and like to work with others to do so. They are loyal and dependable in all areas and tend to put others before themselves.

Advantages: The Supporter's natural inclination to help others makes them highly capable of empathy, and they are often able to notice what people need and want out of their daily lives. They are acutely aware of the emotions of those around them and love helping out when needed. Understanding the full range of emotions in another person comes easy to an ESFJ.

Obstacles: In their occasional blind support for others, this personality type can sometimes be too trusting and leave themselves vulnerable if they aren't careful. It's easy for a Supporter to forget about their own needs in favor of what they can do for someone else. This is not a difficult problem to overcome, though, and simply need to remind themselves every once in a while that their emotions need attention too.

ENFJ (extroversion/intuition/feeling/judging) – Mentor

Definition: The ENFJ is a Mentor by nature, warm and responsible above all else. They are highly attuned to the emotions and motivations of others, and just want to see everyone reach their full potential. Mentors are good leaders and people often look up to them.

Advantages: ENFJs are extremely capable of the highest level of empathy. They can almost always tell when something is bothering a person, and will do everything humanly possible in order to help them fix it. Their understanding of emotions is rooted in a natural open-mindedness and it's easy for a Mentor to see every angle of a situation.

Obstacles: This ease of understanding others' problems often leads to a Mentor feeling obligated to help someone in need, even if it's not their place to help. Sometimes they can even equate the anxiety of others with their own, and will offer their support as a way of making him- or herself feel better.

ENTJ
(extroversion/intuition/thinking/judging)   –
Chief

Definition: ENTJ is the personality type of a Chief. As born leaders, they are decisive and logical individuals who value efficiency in solving problems. They enjoy planning and setting goals for themselves and others.

Advantages: Chiefs are able to understand that emotions are a part of being human, and accept this fact with patience and fairness. If they can reach a similar conclusion through their own logic, the ENTJ has no problem helping others in a tough situation.

Obstacles: It can be difficult for a Chief to be empathetic of others on an emotional level, as they much prefer to let reason govern their choices in life. It will take a significant amount of patience for a Chief to value an emotional approach and resist shutting another person down due to a differing value system.

By this point you should have a better understanding of where you fall on the Empathy spectrum, and the advantages and obstacles of your potential personality type. It's likely that you'll be able to relate to some aspects of your personality "role", while others will feel totally foreign and different from the self you've come to know and love. This is because human beings are unique individuals who can't be generalized into categories without taking into account personal experience and conditioning. For example, an Examiner who has spent a lot of time interacting with a Supporter is much more likely to be capable of empathy than one who is best friends with an Engineer.

These types and their corresponding attributes aren't meant to suggest that you're doomed if your type has less of a knack for understanding emotions than another, and it also isn't suggesting that accessing your own feelings will be easy for anyone. It's simply meant to provide a template of what you might be able to expect in terms of a starting point. Keep in mind what you've learned here so far as we progress into the second section of this book, which is focused on the advantages and disadvantages of being empathetic, as well as solutions for individuals in a variety of situations and locations on the spectrum.

Part II: Solutions for the Empath in You
Benefits of Being Empathic

There are many positive aspects to being empathically sensitive, and it's a trait that some are luckier than others to have. Considering your sensitivity as a gift rather than a curse will help you to acknowledge being an empath in a positive light. We can't change how we experience emotions, and wishing we did so differently is only avoiding the truth and not living to our true potential.

The biggest benefit of being empathic is your ability to give emotional support. People who are sensitive to the pain and suffering of others are more inclined to be able to help identify or solve the problem through the use of their empathic intuition. A source of serenity for the anxious soul is a good kind of person to have around, and people will likely value your presence in their lives. Being there for your friends and family when they need someone to talk to can be rewarding, and may even help you find insight into solving your own difficulties.

Another positive aspect is the amount of energy experienced by those who attract it. The solar plexus chakra, which is in the lower abdomen, is a source of energy that can be used towards creative pursuits, exercise, or any number of positive personal growth tools. Learning to harness this energy efficiently is the challenge that any empath faces in managing the wealth of energy at their fingertips.

With this plethora of energy and increased sensitivity comes an inclination towards creative expression. Whether it's making something artistically or writing or playing music, empaths have a "head start" when it comes to creative pursuits. Expressing yourself is a win-win in that will help take some of the load off of your shoulders and provide a way of seeing things through your own perspective when interacting with others.

Challenges of Being Empathic

No ability comes without its fair share of corresponding challenges, and having an advanced capacity for empathy is no exception. Rather than focusing on these possible obstacles as weights around your ankles, think of them simply as hurdles to overcome and doors to a new, stronger You.

The obvious and most common disadvantage to being empathic is the physical and emotional toll it takes to be a magnet for the emotions and anxieties of others. While people may feel great after spending time with you and having a conversation about the difficulties they're having in any given aspect of their own life, they rarely consider where that anxiety goes once it isn't plaguing them anymore. Knowing your limits in terms of emotional stress is vital in maintaining a healthy lifestyle, and sometimes we have to accept that a stretch of time alone can help us to recharge and balance our own emotions.

It's easy to feel like you have no control over your body when you're constantly bombarded with the emotions of other people. Mindfulness is key in recognizing the difference between your own anxiety and the anxiety of a foreign source. While it may not get rid of the discomfort completely, it can help to know that just because a negative feeling is present in your consciousness doesn't necessarily mean there's a cause for worry in your own life.

An issue that goes along with this loss of control is a fragmented sense of self or potential identity crisis. There is a large amount of pressure that comes with having to constantly differentiate between the varied sources of emotions you feel, and it can lead to a clouded vision of whom you really are. Try to remind yourself that you have the power to define how this sensitivity makes you a unique individual, and not the other way around. It's a part of you; not a flaw or weakness, even if it feels this way at times.

—

Paradoxically, this increased sensitivity to others can feel more like a rift of alienation than a point of contact and connection to other people. Empaths often feel lonely during their unique experience of life, and believe that nobody will understand if they try to explain it. However, keeping these kinds of things bottled up will only add to the trepidation the empath deals with on a daily basis, and realizing that it isn't a load we have to bear ourselves is the first step in coming to terms with this difference of perspective.

Another potential danger of being empathic is falling victim to the exploitation of others for their own gain. This can lead to a lack of trust in the people surrounding an empath; whether their friends, family, and acquaintances have good intentions or not. Voicing concerns about your relationship with a particular person is never a bad idea, in order to make sure both parties are on the same page at all times. A good friend won't take it as a personal attack and will become more aware of your position as a result, thereby helping them to develop their own sense of empathy in the process.

Empathic Self-Protection

Being empathic means having an awareness of the different ways to interact with different people in your life. More than the average person, an empath has to consider their role in individual and group relationships. Knowing who you can really trust and open up to is vital in maintaining emotional balance; as keeping yourself indefinitely closed off from the world will surely wear you down. Having a core group of friends and family who you can let your guard down with is a huge relief from the constant vigilance of protecting yourself in emotional situations.

Family/Best Friends

They should be your ace in the hole when it comes to opening up about your feelings and letting everyone be aware of the sensitivity you deal with on a daily basis. Having a number of people you can always call or spend time with can be a lifesaver on days when the anxiety is overwhelming and solitude doesn't seem like an ideal alternative. It's important not to consider yourself a burden on others, but rather a unique individual with a rare perspective and a lot to offer. If others have trouble seeing this, it's their loss and no fault of your own. Surrounding yourself with positive relationships is important for anyone, but especially for someone with empathic tendencies, where the stakes are higher and every individual social exchange can either be a source of constructive happiness or negative anxiety.

Friends/Acquaintances

The name of the game in terms of interacting with people and groups you may not know as well as the individuals in your comfort zone, is the definition of _boundaries._ Going into new relationships with an open mind is important, but being overly trustworthy from the beginning isn't worth the potential of getting hurt. Spend time with people in one-on-one situations in order to discern how they specifically affect your emotional state, and decide whether or not to trust them based on your observations. It may seem unfair to be so skeptical of others, but there's a difference between being selfish and judgmental, and looking out for your self-preservation.

Acquaintances/Coworkers

It can be tricky to navigate dealing with people you're forced to spend time with, whether it's at work or school, or someone you live in proximity to, or share a routine with. Learning to guard yourself in these kinds of situations is important as it's not always up to you. However, being open with a flexible boss or teacher can be useful in making your experience more comfortable. Avoid working with people who you don't feel good around, but make sure not to be rude about it as this kind of thing could be easily misunderstood. When it comes to relationships inside and outside your friend group, honesty really is the best policy – it's knowing how honest to be that can prove challenging.

Things to Keep in Mind (and Body)

As someone who is trying to manage their overwhelming emotional sensitivity, there are a few things you should know. You might already be privy to this information, or you might not – but what kind of writer would I be if I assumed that kind of stuff? To the people for whom this is old news: bear with me. And to the newbie empaths out there, I hope it helps!

It's not necessary to take responsibility for someone else's pain.
While it might be difficult to avoid feeling guilty when someone you know is having a hard time, it's important to know the difference between being supportive and feeling responsible for them. Chances are good that you aren't the one making them suffer, and it isn't up to you to fix it. Sure, this might be a good opportunity to give them a hug or ask what's bothering them, but don't feel like it's your fault if they are still feeling down after your pep talk. A person must be willing to help him- or herself in order to properly heal, and sometimes there's just nothing you can do or say to replace the slow and painful process of recovery. After all, sadness is a necessary emotion that helps us to value happiness by contrast. We have to accept that there will be instances where time is the only thing that's going to make a difference; and that's okay.

It's always better to confront pain rather than trying to escape it.

Attempting to ignore anxiety is like trying to pull your way out of a Chinese finger trap. The more you struggle against it, the tighter the reeds become and you end up worse off. By taking a deep breath and acknowledging the pain head on, you put yourself in a solid position to release all of that pent up energy inside. You are the one in control, not the emotions that seem to take over your mind and body in a whirlwind of confusion. Your instinctive reactions to escape, repress, and avoid the issue only work to perpetuate the cycle of suffering; which becomes obvious once considered from outside of that vicious cycle. Making the conscious decision to turn around, let yourself feel the fatigue, confusion, and anger is the first step in letting go of the suffering. Similar to the first point, the only way out of the tunnel is through the darkness, which may not even end up being as dark as you had initially thought it would be. Maybe you'll learn a thing or two about yourself in the process, and upon making it out the other side, the light of day will feel brighter and warmer than ever. Just as there is no happiness without sadness, there's no day without the night; no light without the darkness that make us appreciate it.

Realize that you are not immune to projecting feelings onto others.

One of the easiest (and most understandable) responses to pain and suffering is to ignore the fact that we are not alone. Being overwhelmed by others' emotions at all times can be a powerful distraction to the possibility of other people being affected by our own anxiety. It might be hard to imagine, but consider what it must be like to have a conversation with someone who is drowning in the sea of emotions from an entire room full of people; oblivious to their own suffering. Chances are good that conversation is going to leave both parties feeling even more stressed out and uncomfortable than before, and this doesn't help anybody. Carrying the burden of others' emotions doesn't give you an excuse to ignore your own, and even though it might feel impossible to focus on anything else in that moment, the last thing you want to do is perpetuate the cycle, and shove that anxiety onto someone else. By playing the victim and shirking responsibility for your own happiness, you've placed the burden onto everyone around you who probably has less of a clue how to deal with it than you do. To reiterate a previous point, healing only happens when the person in pain is willing to help him or herself. Learning to distinguish the difference between your own feelings and the feelings of others is key here, in order to give yourself as much power to manage your pain as possible, without bringing the pain of others into the mix at the same time.

Know the importance of self-esteem in dealing with empathic tendencies.
It's hard to feel confident and optimistic on the

---

outside when there's a storm brewing in your belly. Understandably, we tend to blame feelings of hopelessness and depression on the excess of stimuli that seems to be giving us anxiety in the first place. But imagine how good it would feel to smile and laugh in spite of that anxiety – to feel true happiness through love and self-respect even when your insides are in turmoil. To trust that you have the strength to overcome that anxiety and, once you do make it through to the other side, knowing it was your own perseverance that got you through it. If you do it once, you can do it again, so it should be easier to beat the pain when the next episode comes along. At the end of the day, it's about how you honestly look at this condition of emotional sensitivity. It is the way things are, and there's no use denying it. You may find it helpful to consider the other side of the coin; the alternative to which is feeling nothing at all. It sounds simple, but considering your empathic tendencies a gift rather than a curse can make all the difference when it comes to self-esteem.

Being an empath is not the same as having empathy.

As we've already touched on briefly in this book, there is a large spectrum when it comes to differentiating between understanding empathy, having empathic tendencies, and identifying as a full-fledged empath. It comes down to the difference between simply having sympathy and knowing real compassion for another person. Having empathy is the ability to see below the surface and understand a situation through someone else's perspective, or a person's behavior; as a result of the situation, or a set of beliefs, feelings, and values that seem foreign to us but come instinctively to someone else. It's really an emotional and intellectual experience more than anything, and nearly everyone has the capacity to feel this understanding, even if it requires a little effort. Being an empath, on the other hand, is a kinesthetic and visceral experience that is felt in a much different way than empathy. For some, empathy can be controlled or shut off. For others this is not the case, and the only choice in the matter is their response to the experience. Both kinds of people have to acknowledge that nobody can possibly know how anyone else is feeling at any given moment – while it may seem decisive for someone to say "get over it" and move past a feeling of anxiety; an empath can't have unrealistic expectations in the understanding of others. It's difficult enough to manage emotions alone, without someone else adding to the stress. So regardless of which side you identify with, it's always better to give the benefit of the doubt and lean towards being supportive rather than skeptical of another individual's experience of pain.

Shielding is not a useful tactic.
The term "shielding" refers to the process of blocking out your emotions in favor of immediate protection, and telling yourself that you'll deal with them a later, more convenient time. The fact

is that there is never a "convenient" time to overcome suffering, and it only serves to perpetuate the pain. It's like using a band aid for a broken bone; it might appear to give us a sense of temporary relief; but it will hurt twice as badly once the distraction wears off. Shielding is a method of resisting energy that exists whether we like it or not, rather than opening ourselves to the experience. It uses the language of victimhood that we know very well by now is counterproductive to healing, and should be avoided if at all costs.

Catharsis and mindfulness are useful tactics. Once we let the experience of empathetic suffering wash over us, the need to cleansing ourselves of this energetic baggage becomes apparent. The task then becomes finding ways to be in touch with your own body to anchor and ground yourself in a state of acute self-awareness. This could come in the form of journaling or writing creatively, a simple act of chronicling your day as a form of reflection and re-experiencing each moment as you review it. Physical techniques like yoga, meditation, or other forms of exercise can also help to develop an awareness of your body by utilizing your muscles to find balance. It might sound silly, but even simple actions like laughing at nothing or screaming into your pillow can help offer some immediate and comforting release. Whatever method you choose to speak with your body and/or mind, it will only help the inner dialogue necessary for managing the empathic

—

experience.

Consider the possibility that everyone has the potential to be an empath.
I know, I know, we've spent so much time differentiating the points on the spectrum; but stick with me for a moment. What if being an empath is the natural state of human beings? If we are all born with the capacity to be in tune with each other's emotions, similar to the way that trees communicate through invisible pheromones and electrical signals? Consider that this ability may be blocked in most people through cultural conditioning, various differences in upbringing, and mass desensitization. Perhaps the ones who are still sensitive have kept something we were all meant to have; and that the poor folks who don't feel so empathically are the ones missing out? Is ignorance really bliss when it comes to emotions?

We'll probably never know the truth about why some people are more emotionally reactive and sensitive than others, but the point is that one way to experience this life is no better or worse than another. In the end, we're all searching for the balance of understanding with one another, and we all have different starting points and paths to traverse in order to get there. It's up to us whether we walk the path alone or in company; staring at the ground or looking together, up into the sky. Regardless of your individual condition, it seems sensible to make the most of your gifts and to share what knowledge and support we can with each other.

Let's take a moment to reiterate a few important points before moving on to more concrete solutions for the balanced and healthy management of your empathic sensitivity.

Benefits
- Considering your sensitivity as a gift rather than a curse will help you to acknowledge your differences from others in a positive light.
- Capability for healing purposes; source of serenity for friends and family.
- Bountiful amounts of energy can be directed towards creative pursuits, mindfulness, and physical exercise.

Challenges
Rather than focusing on these possible obstacles as weights around your ankles, think of them simply as hurdles to overcome and opportunities to a new, stronger You.

The physical and emotional toll it takes to be a magnet for the emotions and anxieties of others.
Solution: Knowing your limits in terms of emotional stress.

Loss of control over emotions and anxiety.

Solution: Recognizing the difference between your own anxiety and the anxiety of others.

Fragmented sense of self or potential identity crisis.
Solution: Remind yourself that you have the power to define how this sensitivity makes you as a unique individual, and not the other way around.

Loneliness in unique experience, alienation from others.
Solution: Open up to others; find support group to rely on, realize it isn't a burden you have to bear alone.

Possibility of falling victim to the exploitation of others for their own gain; loss of trust as a result.
Solution: Voice concerns to foster understanding; provide opportunity for others' development of empathy in the process.

Empathic Self-Protection
Family/close friends:
Having a number of people you can always call or spend time with can be a lifesaver on days when the anxiety is overwhelming and solitude doesn't seem like an ideal alternative.

Friends/acquaintances
Spend time with people in one-on-one situations in order to discern how they specifically affect your emotional state, and decide whether or not to trust them based on your observations.

Acquaintances/coworkers
Learn to guard yourself in situations where you're forced to spend time in proximity with certain people (coworkers, classmates, etc.).

Important to Know

It's not necessary to take responsibility for someone else's pain.

It's always better to confront pain rather than trying to escape it.

You are not immune to the projection of feelings onto others.

Know the importance of self-esteem in dealing with empathic tendencies.

Being an empath is not the same as having empathy.

Shielding is not a useful tactic.

Catharsis and mindfulness are useful tactics.

Consider the possibility that everyone has the potential to be an empath.

Consider the previous information as a collection of preventative techniques to form a basis for

your understanding of being an empa
you've probably noticed, this is more a
mindset than anything else, and staying positi
in terms of the acknowledgement of your
sensitivity will help you to consider these
tendencies as a part of you rather than a set of
obstacles that were randomly imposed upon you
to make your life more difficult. As we continue
on to short-term and long-term solutions for
dealing with anxiety attacks in the moment, as
well as developing and maintaining emotional
balance in between episodes, keep this basis of
positivity in mind and remember you're more
than capable of dealing with being an empath.

Be aware of social anxiety and phobia symptoms.
Knowing the kinds of situations that might trigger an anxiety attack or emotional episode will help you to prepare for the experience and prevent you from being caught off guard. Try to make plans and stick to them whenever possible, and avoid going alone to places or events where you might feel uncomfortable.

Fight the fear of possible embarrassment by taking control over your level of participation in a group setting. This may mean avoiding being the center of attention, or intentionally leaving the comfort zone on your own terms rather than on someone else's. Don't let yourself be pressured into something you know you don't want to do.

Know your emotional limits and when to take a step back.
Knowing when to distance yourself from a particular person or situation making you feel uncomfortable is important in protecting yourself from stress and anxiety. Practice ways to do this without coming off as rude or insulting, to avoid further confrontation and unpleasant interaction. Finding the bathroom or another person, ("I just remembered I have something to tell so-and-so over there, and will catch up with you later!") are

good ways of doing this.

Use grounding techniques to remain in the present moment.
If you do find yourself caught off guard by a situation or setting and feel a loss of control coming on, try to focus on a familiar person or object to keep yourself from getting carried away in the wave of anxiety inside your body. A smile from a friendly face, a gentle squeeze on the hand, or a warm hug can all do the trick, if you're with someone you trust. Carrying a worry stone in your pocket or another small object to rub or fiddle with can also be good ways to bring you back to reality through the experience of a physical sensation.

Find outlets for anxiety overload and ways to keep your mind busy.
Constructing a routine so that your natural state is one of physical and mental balance helps to keep you in a baseline state. This can also be an effective short-term solution to take your mind off of an episode or setback. Methods of personal expression like drawing or writing are great; accessing your creativity and mindfulness at the same time. Physical activities like yoga, meditation, and working out help you to know the way your body works, and how to feel comfortable in your own skin. Exercise will also help you sleep better in general and maintain a healthy metabolism.

Reach out to therapy or support groups if

—

necessary.
Sometimes a sympathetic friend or family member is just not well-equipped enough to help, and someone with formal experience in psychology and emotional distress is needed to make a difference. Finding a group of people to meet with about your anxiety issues can help increase your comfort in social situations, and will remind you that other people experience the same difficulties. You might even make a new friend to share new things with, knowing you're both on the same page.

Now that you have some tools for reducing stress and anxiety, it's time to consider ways to maintain this balance so that you're in a more constant state of equilibrium and prepared to handle any emotional spikes or anxiety attacks.

How to Balance Your Empathy

Set your boundaries.
As we've touched on before, spending too much time and energy on restoring equilibrium for others is another way of ignoring your own needs. In order to help anyone else, you must find your own sense of balance first. Without it, you risk the potential of a "blind leading the blind" type of situation and could end up doing more harm than good for all parties involved.

This goes for emotional/mental boundaries as well as physical ones. Integrating these limits will help to make your anxiety a more tangible, manageable issue; rather than trying to harness it like catching a cloud with a butterfly net.

Bring awareness to your body.
When you sacrifice your own direct experience for someone else's, you lose the awareness that is essential for your personal balance. Acknowledging your own presence in the moment as often as possible will help you to maintain a level head and physical stability. Focusing specifically on your abdominal core or "seat of power" gives you a place to start where excess energy tends to gather and pool. Things like good posture and flexibility help to prevent knots from forming and encourage the smooth flow of energy throughout the rest of your body.

71

Treat the nervous system as an emotional antenna.
It's not uncommon for the mental demands of processing information to catapult your nervous system into overdrive. This can seem to happen out of nowhere and produce a domino effect leading to emotional episodes and panic attacks. Noticing the symptoms of an increased heart rate or "buzzing" sensation in your head can help to stop a breakdown from happening before it starts. Practicing a simple set of breathing techniques to remember in such a moment will help to slow your racing heart and calm you down enough to think clearly.

Regulate the type and amount of intimacy you're exposed to.
It can be difficult to let someone take care of us when we're feeling vulnerable. Getting over this sense of pride to enable receiving treatment turns this vulnerability into a conscious development of your personal space. Being clear about when and where it's okay for someone to touch you is another way to highlight your own control in any kind of relationship, and can be especially helpful for an empath who might be affected more negatively by unexpected contact than others.

Develop a sense of emotional immunity.
Like washing your hands in order to prevent getting sick, practicing emotional "hygiene" will help give you an emotional immune system to fight the invasion of others' anxiety into your

consciousness. Cleansing exercises like deep breathing and brief moments of solitude will strengthen your body's ability to recognize foreign emotion and give you the choice to embrace it or shut it out on your own terms.

Put Feeling to Empathic Practice

In Others

If you find yourself fed up with forgiving others' lack of effort to empathize with your sensitivity, there are things you can do to help nurture the consideration in other people. Teaching your friends and family to be more aware of the emotions they're feeling and giving off, should make your life a little easier, with less of others' emotions to carry as your own. There is also reciprocity in this exchange. Keeping an open mind to techniques you could learn from those who are less emotionally inclined could help you to achieve a personal balance as well.

Volunteering is an especially good way to get someone outside his or her own head for a few hours. Participating in an activity together opens doors for an exchange of experience, and sharing each your views along the way will help you maintain an understanding of multiple perspectives.

Active listening is a big part of this, and consciously trying to understand one another rather than just waiting for your turn to speak will work wonders in developing understanding. Encouraging the curiosity to ask questions instead of waiting for the other to make their way around to your concerns is another way to foster control in social interactions with some is willing to be more empathetic.

In Children

Developing habits of empathy at an early age is a great way to make sure your child will grow up considering the feelings of others and the effect their thoughts and actions can have. Encouraging "empathic imagination" has to do with projecting thoughts and emotions onto people they don't know, animals, or even inanimate objects. By speculating what another being is thinking, the child grows accustomed to a whole range of possible responses. You can never be too transparent with children, so guiding them along every step of the process and taking things slow are good ideas when working on empathy.

In Yourself

This section will be useful for those of you who are looking to develop their own sense of empathy in able to be more considerate of others, or perhaps a close friend or loved one who they know to be highly sensitive. The most important exercise in developing this sensitivity is putting yourself in someone else's shoes as often as possible, and the further that person is from your own comfy slip-ons, the better.

ersations with strangers is a way to conceived notions behind and start is of expectations and judgment. leave your comfort zone in order to o relate to others without the habits usly developed and broaden your emotional horizons. Books and movies are also a great way to embark on "imaginative journeys" that will challenge your expectations and give you a place to start for considering different perspectives, especially if the movie is outside your preferred genre.

Developing empathy in conflict is one of the more difficult situations to exercise patience and understanding. Listening for the needs and feelings of the other person instead of waiting to get your point across is of utmost importance. One way to exhibit empathy is to repeat the points of the person you're talking to before starting in on your own. It will help to make sure you actively absorb what they're saying, adding a layer to your awareness and understanding of where they're coming from.

How to Deal with Narcissistic Individuals

On the opposite end of the spectrum from the empath is the narcissist; exhibiting a blatant disregard for others and a conscious obsession with their own wants and feelings. Under the external shell of self-centeredness and absorption is often a weak inner core of doubt and a lack of self-confidence, making these individuals a volatile danger to everyone around them. They can be manipulative above all else, so taking the skeptical approach is highly recommended. Limiting the amount of emotion they have to work with will give them less of a chance to take advantage of others, so interacting with a narcissist may be one of the few times it would be better to shield yourself and be as stoic as possible.

Dealing with a narcissist at work can be one of the most difficult situations because you are combining an emotionally inflammable individual with an environment you forced to spend extended periods of time in. Things like trying to pitch ideas in a group setting as opposed to one on one with this person can help minimize their power of manipulation and avoid any kind of conflict they might try to incite. Stand up for yourself and resist passing the blame onto others to make sure a narcissistic coworker doesn't get the satisfaction of hurting others for their own gain. Be as neutral as possible around these people to avoid encouraging their grandiose sense of self through the intimidation of others, as well as to keep the volatile under layer of their personality at bay. While it may be hard, remembering that narcissists are indeed people with feelings will help you from overreacting to their behavior. Understanding is a two-way street, and some people will be harder to reach a balance with than others.

Here's an overview of these methods as a quick reference guide:

Stress/Anxiety Reduction Methods, Balance Exercises

Be aware of social anxiety and phobia symptoms.

Know your emotional limits and when to take a step back.

Use grounding techniques to remain in the present moment.

Find outlets for anxiety overload and ways to keep your mind busy.

Reach out to therapy or support groups if necessary.

Develop your boundaries.

Bring awareness to your body.

Treat the nervous system as an emotional antenna.

Regulate the type and amount of intimacy you're exposed to.

Develop a sense of emotional immunity.

Empathic Practice

Teach your friends and family to be more aware of the emotions they're feeling and giving off.

Suggest volunteering as way to get someone outside his or her own head for a few hours.

Encourage the curiosity to ask questions instead of waiting for someone to make their way around to your concerns.

Encourage "empathic imagination" in children to develop good empathic habits of awareness at a young age.

Put yourself in someone else's shoes as often as possible.

Have conversations with strangers to challenge your preconceived notions and judgments.

Leave your comfort zone and force yourself to learn objectively.

Take "Imaginative journeys" in books and movies that will challenge your expectations.

During verbal conflict, repeat the points of the person you're talking to before starting in on your own in order to properly absorb what they're saying by active listening.

Outcomes

As we near the end of our journey toward empathic enlightenment, take the time to acknowledge how far you've already come in dealing with your emotional issues. What used to feel like an impossibly overwhelming condition of constant anxiety is now (hopefully) a manageable character trait that has many benefits, despite the challenges and obstacles that come with it. I know you're capable of living the life you want to and helping others with their own emotional issues, if you choose to do so. The fact that you initiated a search for help in reading this book is the first of many steps in the right direction, and I hope it's been helpful in fostering the beginning of a perspective change. Remember: only you have the power to decide whether your empathic sensitivity is a gift or a curse. Now let's go over the outcomes of this change in outlook.

Part I: So You Think You're an Empath

1. Common Traits of Empathic Individuals

Goal: Gauge where you might fall on the empathy spectrum based on your level of sensitivity towards a number of topics or ideas.

Outcome: An understanding of what specific areas you're sensitive to, and a starting point to finding solutions for managing these sensitivities.

2. Understanding Empathy, Having Empathic Tendencies, and Identifying as an Empath

Goal: Differentiate between these terms; discover the terminology that will help you to categorize your sensitivity; and visualize where that might place you on the empathy spectrum.

Outcome: Ability to put your sensitivity in perspective, and understand the full spectrum of possible emotional experience. Knowledge that things could be even more overwhelming than they already are, and that it is perhaps better to feel too much than not at all.

3. Personality Type as Empathy Indicator

Goal: Learn how the MBTI works and visualize where you might fall in its categorization, discover the advantages and obstacles each personality type might face in managing their empathy.

Outcome: Explanation for your natural inclination towards, or aversion to experiencing empathy and recognizing the emotions of others. Knowledge of solutions make up for the challenges of personality type, and allows you to relate to others of various inclinations.

Part II: Solutions for the Empath in You

4. Benefits of Being Empathic

Goal: Learn to consider your emotional sensitivity as a gift rather than a curse.

Outcome: An optimism that will inform your outlook on possible ways to manage your sensitivity, and make it easier to overcome and live with being empathic.

5. Challenges of Being Empathic

Goal: Prepare yourself for possible obstacles, consider initial solutions for dealing with each. Realize that a positive outlook can transform these challenges from road blocks to opportunities.

Outcome: Knowledge of what to expect in terms of difficulties with managing your emotions, and a more informed approach to conquering these difficulties.

6. Empathic Self-Protection

Goal: Recognize the importance of distinguishing between types of relationships and people, based on your emotional needs.

Outcome: A rationale for maintaining current relationships in regards to your emotional sensitivity, and knowledge of guidelines for cultivating healthy new ones from the beginning. Methods for avoiding people and situations that trigger anxiety episodes or make you uncomfortable.

7. Things to Keep in Mind (and Body)

Goal: Explore methods of confronting your pain, learn the importance of self-esteem, and discover tactics for reducing your discomfort in general.

Outcome: An awareness of common misconceptions towards having empathic tendencies, and a

---

83

set of reminders to prevent setbacks of this awareness.

8. Stress and Anxiety Reduction Strategies

Goal: Learn specific strategies to deal with anxiety attacks and emotional episodes. Discover short-term and long-term solutions for each, and live a comfortable life through your sensitivity.

Outcome: Knowledge of what to do in the case of an episode and how to remain grounded until it passes. Methods for preventing or decreasing the occurrence of these anxiety attacks.

9. How to Balance Your Empathy

Goal: Find ways to maintain an emotional balance in between episodes and reduce the frequency of their occurrence.

Outcome: Longer stretches of time between episodes, more comfort in living a normal life. Healthier mind and body as a result of mental and physical habits and routines.

10. Put Feeling to Empathic Practice

—

Goal: Help others develop their empathic tendencies, discover how to become more empathic if you find yourself on the other end of the spectrum, and explore methods of walking a mile in someone else's shoes.

Outcome: Surrounding yourself with individuals capable of empathic awareness and support and acknowledge the obstacles presented to those on the other side of the spectrum. Understand the benefit of exchanging experiences, in order to understand the possibilities if things were different, and learning to appreciate the way you are.

11. How to Deal with Narcissistic Individuals

Goal: Learn what it means to be a narcissist, how to recognize them in relationships, and possible ways of dealing with these kinds of people without being taken advantage of.

Outcome: Knowledge of preventative measures to avoid being caught off guard and taken advantage of when dealing with narcissists.

Well, my empathic friend, it seems this is the end of the road in terms of our journey through the words of this book. I hope the previous pages have helped to change what used to be your ball-and-chain emotions into wings of opportunity. You are now more equipped to manage the sensitivity that makes you such a unique individual with infinite potential to help yourself and others. You understand your personality in a more intimate manner and this will help you to communicate your feelings more efficiently and for positive results. You know how to protect yourself when you need to and, more importantly, know how to avoid the necessity to "protect" yourself at all.

If there are any lingering doubts as to whether your sensitivity is a good thing, remember this: without empathy, ours would be planet of narcissists, each only able to comprehend his or her own emotions, and everyone looking out expressly for themselves. People like you have the ability to show a world of individuals how to relate to one another on a deeper and more meaningful level. You're the role models in everyone else's emotional education, and I know you can live up to the challenge. I've learned so much from my friendship with Laura, and I wish everyone had somebody like her to help them be more in touch with a side of themselves that society often confuses as weakness. But she knows, and I know, and now you know, that it's only a weakness if you let them get the best of you. The only difference between Zeus's thunderbolt and Achilles' heel is the perspective of the person telling the story. So go on, and be the empathic hero you were born to be!

FREE DOWNLOAD

INSIGHTFUL GROWTH STRATEGIES FOR YOUR PERSONAL AND PROFESSIONAL SUCCESS!

88

You may also like...
EMOTIONAL INTELLIGENCE SPECTRUM
EXPLORE YOUR EMOTIONS AND IMPROVE YOUR
INTRAPERSONAL INTELLIGENCE
BY JOSHUA MOORE AND HELEN GLASGOW

Emotional Intelligence Spectrum is the one book you need to buy if you've been curious about Emotional Intelligence, how it affects you personally, how to interpret EI in others and how to utilize Emotional Quotient in every aspect of your life.

Once you understand how EQ works, by taking a simple test, which is included in this guide, you will learn to harness the power of Emotional Intelligence and use it to further your career as you learn how to connect with people better.

You may also like...
MAKE ROOM FOR MINIMALISM
A PRACTICAL GUIDE TO SIMPLE AND
SUSTAINABLE LIVING
BY JOSHUA MOORE

Make Room for Minimalism is a clear cut yet powerful, step-by-step introduction to minimalism, a sustainable lifestyle that will enable you to finally clear away all the physical, mental and spiritual clutter that fills many of our current stress filled lives. Minimalism will help you redefine what is truly meaningful in your life.

Eager to experience the world of minimalism? Add a single copy of **Make Room for Minimalism** to your library now, and start counting the books you will no longer need!

FN№

Presented by French Number Publishing
French Number Publishing is an independent
publishing house headquartered in Paris, France
with offices in North America, Europe, and Asia.
FN№ is committed to connect the most promising
writers to readers from all around the world.
Together we aim to explore the most challenging
issues on a large variety of topics that are of
interest to the modern society.

FN№
